Goddess
and
Witch

Acknowledgement is due to the following publications in which many of these poems previously appeared:
The Salmon; Writing in the West (Connaught Tribune); Cyphers; The Poetry Ireland Review; The Honest Ulsterman; Bad Seeds; The Simon Anthology; The Irish Socialist; Oxford Poetry; Die Horen; In Galway; Maryland Poetry Review; Visions; Folio International; Echo Room; Quarto; Midland Review; Gown Literary Supplement.

□□□□□□□□

Typeset and Designed by Nova Print, Galway.
Printed by Clodoiri Lurgan Teo.
Bound by Kenny's Fine Binding.
Cover photo by Anne Kennedy.

□□□□□□□□

ISBN 0 948339 31 4 Hardcover £9.00
ISBN 9 948339 32 2 Softcover £5.95

□□□□□□□□

Produced with the assistance of Galway Borough Council, and patrons:
The Waterfront Bar, Galway, TGT Computer Software, Spiddal, Co. Galway.

Salmon Publishing,
Auburn, Upper Fairhill, Galway.

Goddess on the Mervue Bus

Witch in the Bushes

Introduction

Rita Ann Higgins' goddess and witch live
around the corner from each other. The
goddess' beauty might be awe-inspiring but she
travels by bus to her council house; the witch
might be watchful and mercurial, but she is
trying to solve her financial and marital
problems. Both have husbands, children,
mothers-in-law, aunts, grandmothers, fathers,
both have problems with the rent man, their best
friends, the blanket man, the husband, the
children, the mother-in-law, both have fights
with nosy neighbours, community welfare
officers, macho types and tattooed men with
ratlike dogs. They smoke too much, use strong
language, play bingo, get drunk, sometimes
they despair of the lovelessness of their
marriages and retreat into a world of their own
and sometimes they take flight from the
monotony of everyday existence in dreams of
villas and an easier life, more money, less
family, more fulfilment, or simply a man who
talks to clouds. They are not "spun from rolled
gold" or the web of myth but made of flesh and
blood and the qualities that enable them to carry
on are resilience, wit and irrepressible joie de
vivre. They are the alter ego of the poet and

every woman who inhabits and is aware of the present, the Ireland of today with all its problems of unemployment, poverty, emigration. Being allowed to come to life in these perceptive and witty poems, they act out the interplay of their aspirations and disappointments, their strengths and weaknesses before the backdrop of constriction through marriage, lack of opportunity, old age or sickness.

Rita Ann Higgins is a solitary phenomenon in the literary scene in Ireland in that she turns her critical attention especially to the causes of social ills and never fails to take the side of the powerless and humiliated with energy and commitment. She possesses a fine nerve for tyranny and transgression, whether it shows up in the guise of institutional, class, or male power. Remarkably unimpressed by literary fashions and dictates she deals with subjects usually considered unfit for poetry. Her poems are informed by compassion, her style is sharp, laconically brief and full of colloquialisms and slang. Together with her anarchical humour and her honesty this produces an irresistible mixture as the sales figures of her two collections have shown. And it is a particular quality of her appeal that it transcends all barriers of age, class and nationality. No matter where she reads or is read - in schools or universities, women's groups or prisons, arts festivals or political meetings, in Ireland, England, America, Germany or Hungary, the response is unanimously one of interest and delight. As one student of literature put it after a reading in the university of Tübingen: "It was a revelation to me that poetry could be anything other than ponderous and difficult, but that it could be direct, enlightening and entertaining."

This edition, collected from "Goddess on the Mervue Bus" and "Witch in the Bushes", therefore comes just in time to meet the persistent demand for more from Rita Ann Higgins.

Eva Bourke.

Goddess
on the
Mervue Bus

Consumptive in the Library

About you:
you carry a kidney donor card,
not yet filled in,
a St. Christopher's round your neck
on a brown shoe lace,
(to ward off demons and politicians),
memories of Sweet Afton,
the racing page from the Daily Express
and an unsociable cough.

About me:
I carry illusions
of becoming a famous poet,
guilt about that one time in Baltinglass,
fear that the lift will stop at Limbo,
a slight touch of sciatica
plus an anthology of the Ulster poets.

Unlike your peers
you will not take warmth
from cold churches or soup kitchens,
instead, for long periods, you will
exasperate would-be poets with illusions,
in the reference room of the Galway County
Library.

I started with Heaney,
you started to cough.
You coughed all the way to Ormsby,
I was on the verge of Mahon.

Daunted, I left you the Ulster Poets
to consume or cough at.

I moved to the medical section.

Evangeline

Evangeline,
God help her,
reacts to macho men,
who in the end
expect her to survive
on the draught
of far-flung embraces,

not interested in
her food-mixer philosophies,
her many ways
with crux pastry.

Only wanting
what she can never
give freely.

Look Evan, through
your stainless net curtains,
another far-flung embrace -
take it,

opium for the dead
self that leads
to seven second security.

She had notions,
some dreary Tuesdays,
about swish red
sports cars
and a villa
off the something
coast of France.

She saw herself
in a plunging neckline,
offering her condolences
to Anthony Quinn
Lee Marvin types.

Much later
that same lifetime,
when the kids are asleep,
she crawls out
of her apron
pocket and meets herself
for the first time that day
in the eyes of Martha Glynn,
ten Silk Cut
and a small white sliced.

"Will we see you
on the bingo bus
a Friday, Martha G?"

"I wouldn't miss it
for the world."
And out of her mouth
came all the eights,
and she brought
laughter to all
in Folan's shop
for the second
time this month.

The Day Bridie O'Flaherty
was Made Mayor
(for Jennifer)

Your sister was upstairs
chanting to god Springsteen
on the headphones.

Your father
was in the Labour Exchange
waiting for the statues to move.

Your ageing mother
was watching four dead mackerel
on the draining-board, hoping they would fillet
themselves.

And you my love
were cutting grass
with the new scissors
we got free from Family Album
with your father's moccasins
that were never paid for.

And the dollar swerved two point two cents shy
of the pound.

Mrs. McEttigan

No coincidence was this,
it was arranged by God,
you would say.

Me, posting a letter.
You, you were just there.

You, from somewhere in Ulster,
I loved your accent.
Me, from somewhere in space,
you loved my mother.

You always said the same thing
"Your mother is in Heaven,
she was a saint, God be good to her."

You lifted your eyes.

You, with the posh brooch,
two stones missing, your Mass hat.

I was just there.

Don't ever die Mrs. McEttigan
I need to see you outside the Post Office
sending glances to a saint.

7

Tommy's Wife

She wasn't always this bitter,
I knew her when she sang in pubs.

She was younger then and free,
a happy life she spent.

Working in Woolworths,
she kept herself well. Blue eye shadow.

She married for the sake of the kid.
A lot of envelopes she received. The day.

It started out well for her
the family stood by her then.

Tommy looks strong, many friends,
likes Guinness, sex and unemployment.

She lost blue eye shadow first year,
Sara now five months, teething hard.

She didn't sing in pubs anymore,
she wasn't as friendly as before.

The other three children didn't delay,
she remembered wearing blue eye shadow.

The coal man hated calling now,
he didn't understand her anger.

Tommy looks strong, many friends,
likes Guinness, sex and unemployment.

Unnecessary Work
(for Bernie)

Sunday evening
we walked
unwanted calories
into the prom
for leisure.

Our duty now
homeward-bound
to visit the mother's grave.

On an unkempt plot nearby
a community of pink carnations
overpowers me.

"You won't have luck for it,"
my sister said.

Later on they stood
in a black Chinese vase
accompanied by
one blooming spike
of white gladiolus
the cat had broken off.

Their agreeable essence
adds life to this room.

10

I mime a hurried
prayer for the repose
of the soul of
Mary Elizabeth Cooke.

What is a Canary?

Hippolyta O'Hara
would like to own
a mare called Bella.

But where would she keep her,
she lives in a housing estate,
no mares named Bella allowed.

Hippolyta O'Hara
would like to own
a minotaur called Harry.

But where would she keep him,
she lives in a housing estate,
no minotaurs named Harry allowed.

Hippolyta O'Hara
would like to own
a crocodile called Leonard.

but where would she keep him,
she lives in a housing estate,
no crocodiles named Leonard allowed.

Hippolyta O'Hara
would like to own
a canary called Dominico,

but the cat would eat him.

"What about the housing estate?"

A canary is a canary
in a housing estate
or in a bishop's house.

The cat is the problem.

Work On

Nostalgia takes me back -
the shirt factory toilet.

Where country girls met
and sucked cigarette ends on Monday mornings.

Sunday night was discussed, the Ranch House,
his acreage, physique and the make of his car.

Precisely they swayed to and fro,
tannoy blasted sweet lyrics, their hero.

Two jived to the beat, two killed the smoke
and seven sank further into hand-basins.

Boisterous laughter echoed and betrayed lost time.
"Back to work girls," supervisor sang.

A thousand buttonholes today.

A thousand Ranch House fantasies the weekend.

Work On.

The Apprentices

Daily they perch
during factory lunchtimes
on their man-made Olympus.

Who will attempt to pass
through their veil of lust unscathed
by Henry Leech-along's recital
of his nine favourite adjectives?

Hardly the unprotected townie
shielded only by the active ingredients
of a lifetime's venial sins.

Maybe some young one from the Tech.,
the brazen Bridget variety -
mother in a home,
father in a bottle.

Hey you! Wearers of brown acrylic pullovers,
a yellow stripe across your chest-bone
means your mother is still alive,
think not of other people's undertones,
of milk-white flesh, of touching thighs.

AnCo never trained you for this.

Stay awhile Pavlovian pets, fill your sights
with more ambitious things,
like when your apprenticeship ends
and you are released on the world
a qualified this or that.

Right now you are an apprentice's echo,
know your station.

The Syrup of Longevity

"Awful about poor Mr. Carney,
only fifty,
wife and ten kids left behind.
Plenty of exercise and a good
clean diet that's what we need."

"Don't gimme no tripe about them
Air Rubex, my own father
lived to be ninety
not a day's labour in him.
No single day passed that
he didn't colour his egg with
a generous teaspoon of salt.
If his mutton stew didn't have
at least four inches of grease
relaxing on top of it
he wouldn't put a tooth in it.
He'd take ash from a dead man's lips,
he drank poteen every day of his life.
The day before he died
he sat up in the bed and had a working-man's
helping of mutton stew.
His mind went years ago
but that's neither here nor there,
didn't he live to see nicely?"

Annaghmakerrig

At Annaghmakerrig in the semi-dark
you might see things moving
in the trees
if you didn't have your wits akimbo.

Once in a dream I saw Tyrone Guthrie,
in his good suit, fishing green sausages
out of the duck pond.

I tried hard not to see
the four grisly ghouls lashing
the seven swinging cats with their bad breath.

The little black demon with no arse
was not really there at all
nor did he devour six toasted mice
dipped in aubergine sauce.

It's an absolute lie to say
that five truncated gobelinus
did the two-hand-reel in the foyer
each evening before dinner.

I didn't sleep well at Annaghmakerrig.

Power Cut

Black-out excitement, enchanting,
chasing shadows up and down.

Delirious children play scary
monsters, the walls laugh back.

Father Bear sleeps it off,
dreams of good westerns.

Mother Bear thinks it cultural,
collects young, reads by candle shade.

Siblings content, maternal wing snug,
drifting softly, land of milk and honey.

Father Bear slept enough, weary of culture,
"Try the lights upstairs," he shouts.

Mother Bear switches on. Another culture
shock,
westerns, yoghurt and the late news.

Poetry Doesn't Pay

People keep telling me
"Your poems, you know,
you've really got something there,
I mean really."

When the rent man calls, I go
down on my knees, and through
the conscience box I tell him,

This is somebody speaking,
short distance, did you know
I have something here with my poems?
People keep telling me.

"All I want is fourteen pounds
and ten pence, hold the poesy."

But don't you realise
I've got something here.

"If you don't come across
with fourteen pounds and ten pence soon
you'll have something at the side of the road,
made colourful by a little snow."

But.

"But nothing,
you can't pay me in poems or prayers
or with your husband's jokes,
or with photographs of your children
in lucky lemon sweaters
hand-made by your dead Grand Aunt
who had amnesia and the croup.

I'm from the Corporation,
what do we know or care about poesy,
much less grand amnostic dead aunts."

But people keep telling me.

"They lie.

If you don't have fourteen pounds
and ten pence, you have nothing
but the light of the penurious moon."

It's About Time

One day a car pulled up,
the driver asked me the way to Tuam.

I replied,
"Sir, do you know
that where Tuam was yesterday it no longer is today."

The following day a car pulled up,
the driver asked me, "Was there a way to Tuam?"

I replied,
"Sir, do you not know that where Tuam was yesterday
it can no longer be today."

On the third day a car pulled up,
the driver asked me, "Where are you today?"

"Sir," I said,
"Today I am in Tuam and it is four minutes to ·
                                        midnight."

"Madam," said he,
"You've got the right time, but you're in the wrong
                                        place."

Goddess on the Mervue Bus

Aphrodite
of the homely bungalow,
cross curtains,
off-white Anglia at the side.

Your father
(who is no Zeus)
turns old scrap
into rolled gold
nightly from memory,

looks down on you
from his scrap mountain,
hurling forks of caution
about the tin-can man

who fumbles in the aisle
of the Mervue bus,
longing for the chance
of a throwaway smile,
a discarded bus ticket.

O Goddess on the Mervue bus,
no scrap dealer fashioned
you from memory or want,
you were spun from golden
dust, a dash of dream.

Enslaver of mortals,
you choose me.

Once when you yawned
I envisioned myself
sitting cross-legged
on a lonely molar
waiting for the crunch.

Lizzie Kavanagh

There's nothing wrong
with Lizzie Kavanagh,
'Kavvy' for short,
she has that coat
for ages.

It's maroon imitation fur,
extras include
one leatherette belt.

When it was new
she only wore it
to her mother's
and Quinnsworth.

Now she wears it
everywhere, she says
it brings her luck
once she didn't have
it on at bingo and
'never been kissed'
was called and she
only needed one number
for a full house,
after that she swore -

it was definitely the coat.

There's a comfortable
depression on the seat
of it from travelling
on the Shantalla bus
to see her sister-in-law.

She says she'd be lost
without Aggie -
that's her sister-in-law,
and mother -
that's her mother.

There's nothing wrong
with Lizzie Kavanagh,
she just likes bingo,
her mother, Aggie -
that's her sister-in-law,
and maroon imitation -
that's her coat.

Secrets

Secrets are for keeping
not for hiding,
the spines of wardrobes
will talk, sooner or later.

Keep your secrets in your heart,
in hip joints,
between folds of flesh,
or under rotting ulcers.

Never tell best friends,
in time their minds will leak
from old age or too much whiskey.

Don't succumb to pleas of
"I swear I'll never tell,"
eleven will know within the hour.

Don't ever tell priests.

Keep well clear of burning bushes,
investigative mothers-in-law
with egg-shell slippers
and Dundee cake.

Never tell the living dead.

Be on the look-out
for lean neighbours
who slither between hedges
and pose as ant-eaters.

They're really secret stealers in disguise.

As for keeping a diary,
when you're gone
for entertainment, on wet days
and after funerals,
your nearest and dearest
will read it aloud with relish.

Try blushing with clay between your teeth.

The Test

Iquanidae Londis,
a witch doctor with the Regional,
she loves her job.
Her credentials she keeps
where her heart used to be,
it reads *Gut Snipper*.
A vocation for it you might say,
if you had the guts left.

I sampled the test once,
the event I hid deep in the layers of my liver.
One scarred afternoon two years wiser
I collided with witch doctor,
one look into her mad scarlet eyes
brought the whole event nearer the floor.

"Listen, "she said, "there's nothing to it,
I just ram this little off-white tube
forcibly down your stingy little oesophagus,
wriggle it around awhile,
say forty-five mins multiplied by five.

There's a small, sharp, well-dressed blade
at the top of it,
as soon as it attaches itself to your shapely
virginal gut and I see that it's got a piece

of you between its teeth,
I'll just give a little tug with all my sincerity
and up she'll come with gut in hand, hopefully.
Or else we'll have to go again."

So we went again, and on the seventh day I enquired,

"Am I or am I not?"

"Listen, medical card number 64279,
you are no coeliac
but you have the loveliest looking
large intestine I've ever had fourteen snips of.
Go forth and be proud."

All Buckled Up
in the Industrial Estate

Count them buckles,
stack them high.

In rows of boredom
the mind drips,
esteem leaks
all the way
to your fag packet.

We count in rivers and riddles,
we smoke our own.

(Midday Chant)
　　　Count them buckles
　　　stack them high
　　　make them beauties scrape the sky.
(End of Chant)

Time out for lunch and human behaviour.
Thirty minutes of darkness to buckle down.

"What have you?"
"Easy singles."
"Are you easy?"
"I'm simple."

"Me too."
"Who do you want to be when you grow down?"
"A banjaxed buckle."

"Me too."

Lotus Eater from Bohermore

Death is the end of life; ah! why
Should life all labour be?
Lord Tennyson

Salmon-ways of life hold little scenery
for this ageing man in search of employment;
sit-about on an oil rig, his fantasy -
but the rig would have to come to Mohammed
c/o Silver Dollar Amusement Arcade.

Badly in need of a pocket watch,
his mottos etched on an empty wallet.
No sign of the crock of gold -
it would be the wrong currency anyway.

His swollen brain's exhausted
with fantasies of the big break -
nearly always it's an arm or a leg,
never the winning grin
of the Pakistani dealer on the blackjack table.

Philosophies he could sell you,
his dreams he gives away,
but never his place in the dole queue -
it's his security, a high price to pay.

The German for Stomach

(for Eva)

I was waiting for the twenty-past
in the rain, trying to think
of the German for stomach.

While I was racking
I took time out for
a stew fantasy.
When a blue Merc pulled
out in front of a brown Mini,
I had stew fantasy interruptus.

The man in the brown Mini
was blue and furious
but he didn't let on.
Poor Rex later that day.

The blue Merc made me think
of blue skies and blue seas,
then it came to me,
Bauch, that's it, *der Bauch*.
I said it to myself all the way home
except when I passed the graveyard,
time for another stew fantasy.

I got off near Kane's butchers.
Inside they were discussing

the gimp and colour of Sean Sweeney's
duodenum when the doctor opened him.
They called it the Northern Province.

It was on the tip of my tongue
and out it tumbled,
"*Bauch* is the German for stomach."

His wife said,
"Are you sure you don't want
a carrier bag for that, loveen?"

I could see that
the butcher was overwhelmed,
he wanted to shout
"Lapis Lazuli, Lapis Lazuli,"
but instead he said,

"You wouldn't put a dog out in it."

Almost Communication

My father just passed me
in his Fiat 127;
I was cycling my bicycle 'Hideous.'

They stopped at O'Meara's
for the Connacht Tribune.
As I passed I shouted
"road hog" in the window.

The occupants laughed.

Before this he owned
a Renault 12;
we called it the
'Ballyhaunis cow killer.'

Later we met outside the sister's,
"Wouldn't you think
he'd buy you a decent bike, the miser."

"If he had your money," I said
and we laughed.

The neighbours with their ears
to the rose bushes
think that we're great friends.

I haven't seen his eyes for years.

The Benevolent Coat Saver in Black

In the doorway of our shop this ebon nun
declared it, "Something to save my good coat.

The size doesn't matter but the colour, yes,
it must be a dark shade of black.

This seems adequate, but yellow,
it won't match the colour of my faith.

My faith is black, as black as a crow,
I'm saving my good coat. Did I mention.

This, a bit smockish, too wide,
much room for secrets, not allowed."

"It suits you grand,
blends in darkly with your glance.

It's yours for a prayer, will you have it?"
"No, it's the wrong colour black!"

"You have a merciful back to save your good coat,
will you save mine as well?"

Middle-Aged Irish Mothers

Germinating sopranos in conservative head squares
are the middle-aged Irish mothers in heavy plaid
coats, who loiter after Mass in churches

> *Lord make me an instrument of your peace;*
> *Where there is hatred, let me sow love;*

to light candles for the Joes and Tommies of the
drinking world, the no-hopers, that they might pack it in,
if it's the will of God,

> *Where there is injury, pardon;*
> *Where there is discord, union;*

to pray for Susan's safe delivery, Bartley's gambling,
Mrs. Murray's veins, that they would not bother her
so much, not forgetting Uncle Matt's shingles.

> *Where there is doubt, faith;*
> *Where there is despair, hope;*

Soon, not out of boredom, they will move diagonally
                                                    through
their cruciform sanctuary to do the Stations
in echoing semi-song whispers,

We adore thee O christ we bless thee, because by
thy cross thou hast redeemed the world

sincere pleas to dear Jesus, that the eldest might get
off with a light sentence, pledges of no more smoking,
and guarantees of attendance at the nine Fridays,

Where there is darkness, light;
Where there is sadness, joy;

finally, for the Pope's intentions, Mr. Glynn's brother-
in-law,
the sweeps ticket that it might come up,
but only if it's the will of God,

O Sacred Heart of Jesus, I place
all my trust and confidence in thee.

I like these middle-aged Irish mothers, in heavy plaid
coats,
one of them birthed me on the eve of a saint's feast day,
with a little help from Jesus and his Sacred Heart.

I tell you most solemnly, anything you ask for
from the father he will grant in my name.

39

Ode to Rahoon Flats

O Rahoon, who made you
to break the hearts
of young girls with
pregnant dreams

of an end terrace,
crisp white clothes
lines and hire purchase
personalities?

You don't care if her
children crawl into her
curved spine,
distort her thinking.

You put Valium on a
velvet cusion
in the form of a
juicy, red apple.

Rahoon, why are you
so cruel to young
husbands, hooked on
your butter voucher

bribes? If you crumbled
would it take three days
or would the ground swallow
you up, payment for your sins?

Old Friend

Upstairs in Powells our chance encounter,
it must have been fifteen years.

Today made her old, she trembled here.
Outside, the sun made flesh in cars uncomfortable.

On hay-making summers gone by her slow words,
                                        reminiscing,
"We worked you hard and you only a nipper.

And how's Carmel? I remember the day she was
                                        christened,
I cycled four miles in the rain."
She was my mother's best friend, 'a good neighbour'
echoed in that inner distance where the veins began.

Her black mantilla was too tight,
she didn't seem to mind, he was worth it.

"It was my younger brother,
at seventy he was taken. Cancer," she whispered.

She gave a pound to the children to share,
"Your husband's hair is lovely."

An old tear trickled and we almost hugged,
"I'll see you again, please God."

She Never Heard
of Cromwell

When I worked there
I thought she knew everything.

When she walked
her buttocks screamed,

"I know everything."

Years later I came back.

"I'll have a sly coffee
behind a newspaper and
a slice of your best
wisdom, well done."

A patron asked for
Chicken Maryland,
and who was Cromwell?

Years later
when she returned
from Maryland, she said,

"I never heard of Cromwell,
all meals are served with chipped potatoes."

The Long Ward

I have never seen
an old woman
eating an orange.

The long ward
for the old
and sometimes
the odd appendix.

The long ward
for crack,
for prayer,
a joke, a song
and sometimes pain.

In the long ward
Silvermints are
shared and returned
with photographs of
"My second eldest"
or "This one is in Canada."

Some come to visit,
to care, to love,
few to count acres
in old women's eyes.

In the long ward
it pleases when
the priest passes
your bed.

In the dead of night
a cry for somebody's son.
No welcome for the grey
box that comes to call.

Thin legs you see,
smiling mothers
in new Dunnes dressing gowns,
new slippers,
boxes of tissues
they would never use at home.

Always one to joke
about the black doctor,
always one to complain
about the cold tea, no ham.

An eye on the clock,
a hand on the rosary beads,
pain well out of sight.

The loved grandchildren
embrace good-looking oranges
and ancient smiles.

44

God-of-the-Hatch Man

*(for Community Welfare Officers
everywhere)*

Smoking and yes mamming,
snoozing in the fright
of his altered expression,
caused always by the afternoon.

Tepid water sipper, coffee glutton,
pencil pointer, negative nouner,
God-of-the-hatch man, hole in the wall.

We call religiously every Thursday,
like visiting the holy well,
only this well purports to give you things
instead of taking them away.

Things like scarlatina, schizophrenia,
migraine, hisgraine but never your grain,
lockjaw and wind, silicosis,
water on the knee, hunger in the walletness.

We queue for an hour or three,
we love to do this,
our idea of pleasure.
Then whatever-past what-past he likes,
he appears.

Tepid water sipper, coffee glutton,
pencil pointer, negative nouner,
God-of-the-hatch man, hole in the wall.

He gives us money and abuse,
the money has a price,
the abuse is free.

"Are you sure your husband isn't working?"
"Are you sure grumbling granny is quite dead?"
"Are you sure you're not claiming for De Valera?"
"Are you sure you count six heads in every bed?"

Hummer of Andy Williams tunes,
most talked about man in the waiting room,
tapper of the pencil on the big brown desk.

God-of-the-hatch man, hole in the wall.
God-of-the-hatch man, hole in the wall.

Mona

Mona doesn't die here
anymore, she lives
in a house at the back
of her mind.

Some place small,
cosy and warm,
fully detached,
a single storey,
with no gable ending,
a high wall
but no door.

Away from
tenants' associations,
rent man's,
poor man's,
light bills,
heavy bills,
free newspapers,
and six-year-old perpetrators on skates.

When she was here
she was afraid
of salutations,
candied appreciations,

of tendon squeezing
politicians
who didn't care.

In supermarkets
she was tricked by
pennies off here,
free holidays over there,
buy three and get
anxiety for nothing.

She was a coupon saver,
she saved them
but they never saved her.

Mona doesn't die there
anymore, she lives
in a shed at the back
of her house.

Some place small,
cosy and warm,
a high wall
but no door.

Sunny Side Plucked

We met outside
the seconds chicken
van at the market.

He was very American,
I was very married.

We chatted about
the home-made marmalade
I bought two miles
from home.

He said the eggs were big,
I said he'd been eating
his carrots.

"Do you always buy
seconds chickens?"

"Only when I come late."

The witch in me
wanted to scramble
his eggs.

The devil in him
wanted to pluck
my chicken.

We parted
with an agreement
written by the eyes.

Witch in the Bushes

Men with Tired Hair

On a bank holiday Monday in Galway,
you can see old men
sitting on window sills in Prospect Hill.

Time is not a factor here,
only images pleasing and displeasing
to the men with tired hair.

Despite this easiness with life,
there is a waiting, a look out
in anticipation of something.

The looking up and down continues;
The awaited stimulus always comes.

Days it's a young woman.
Streets it's a fire.
Years it's news of a tragedy in far off Dublin.

It's all because
We're Working Class
(for Michael A.)

Through them
you could see
no rhyme reason
or gable end;
that coal bag washer
and grass eater
from the Shantalla clinic
prescribed them.

Burn your patch
he said
and be a man;
slip these on
and see into
the souls of men;
and our Ambrose
walked into
the gable end
and his life
was in splinters
thereafter.

All he really needed
was to rest his lazy eye
for a few months
and the wrong eye
would right itself.

54

It's like having your leg
tied behind your back
for six years
then suddenly have it released
and be told,
go now and break dance
on a tight rope.

It's all because we're working class;
if we lived up in Taylor's Hill
with the coal bag washers
and grass eaters,
do you think for one minute
they would put
them big thick spy glasses on your child?

Not a tall
not a fuckin' tall;
they'd give ya them film star glasses
with the glitter on them,
just as sure
as all their metallic purple wheelbarrows
have matching cocker spaniels
they would;

fuckin' coal bag washers
and grass eaters
the whole fuckin' lot of them; and
it's all because we're working class.

Secret Lovers

They choke
spare minutes,
burgle glances,
burn each other
with hot
passionate kisses,
miss each other
painfully.

When they meet
in the band room
they fall
to the floor
in a snake-like embrace.

Neither of them
smoke, drink,
or drop acid.

The Rat-Catchers
(for Christy)

Their flexible
and benevolent teeth
shine all the way
to Crock-well.

They are related
however distantly,
they will help
they will save him
from the mire,
he may well fall
but it will not be in muck
not while they have
a distant cousin claim on him.

They don't see
that his enemy
·has him by the scruff,
for all their books
and their fact full eyebrows
and their jaws full of greasy hope.

When they call
he will tell them
through the slit in their genes
down to their

distant cousined tailshirts,
that he will be
man enough
to get help for himself
when he can no longer
tell his own front door
from the rats
who dance in his pockets,
until then

he will drink on.

She is not Afraid of Burglars
(for Leland B.)

It's lunchtime
and he's training the dog again.
He says to the dog in a cross voice,
"Stay there"
The dog obeys him.

When he goes home
he forgets to leave the cross voice
in the green where he trains the dog
and spits out unwoven troubles
that won't fit in his head.

He says to his wife,
"Stay there"
His wife obeys him.
She sees how good he is with the dog
and how the dog obeys his cross voice.

She boasts to the locals,
"I would never be afraid of burglars
with my husband in the house."

The locals, bursting for news, ask her,
"Why would you never be afraid of burglars
with your husband in the house?"

She calls a meeting at Eyre Square
for half three that Saturday.
Standing on a chair, wiping her hands
on her apron, she explains.

"One day," she says, in a cross voice,
"the dog disobeyed my husband
and my husband beat him across the head
with a whip made from horse hair.

That is why I am not afraid of burglars
with my husband in the house."

The K.K.K. of Kastle Park

At a K.K.K. meeting
in Kastle Park
you could
walk into a dark garden
void of roses
or an after-Easter lily
but reeking with thorns,

briars too
that smoked
and choked
with shouts of
"Get them out
we don't want them,
they're dirty,
cut off their water."

These briars
have big brothers
and heavy-bellied husbands
(who are really thistles)

who know only
about foam-backed carpet
and curtains
that go up and down

with a string.
These prickly thistles
have roots
in other parts of town,
where they never saw
foam-backed carpet
or curtains
that went up and down
with a string.

Now these deep roots
spoke often
at peak thistle times
about the lessers
who are dirty
on the outside,

of them they warned,
"My prickly sons,
you are better
than this sort,

so if they cross
your path
step on them
nip them in the bud,
know you are superior."

And the thorny briars
who smoked and choked
had cacti problems
with their male thistles
and with money
and with awkward shaped light bills.

Sometimes these thistles
chased other briars;
some played cards
with the briar money
others played the horses
the evil ones drank jungle juice.

All the time
the anger
of the frustrated briars
and thistles
was building up
under the stairs
in the houses
with the foam-backed carpet
and the curtains
that went up and down
with a string.

And the
heavy-bellied husbands
of the thorny briars,

sent out
in the dead of night
their children,
to inform
all the other
briars and thistles
about the Midnight Court at Kastle Park,

where they would
nip in the bud,
the lessers
their fathers spoke about
at peak thistle times.

And all
the under-stair anger
burst forth
and was spread unevenly
over the streets
and over the caravans,

and a chalice full
seeped into
a hive-shaped chapel.

After that
all the thistles and briars
went home
and danced
on their foam-backed carpet,

and pulled the string
and the curtains
came down and down
(but no one took any notice)

And they all
slept soundly
knowing they did a good job,
nipping the lessers
in the bud.

It Wasn't the Father's Fault

His father
hit him
with a baseball bat
and he was
never right since.

Some say
he was never right
anyway.

Standing
behind the kitchen table
one Sunday before Mass
his mother said,

"If Birdie Geary
hadn't brought
that cursed baseball bat
over from America,

none of this would have happened."

The Did-You-Come-Yets
of the Western World

When he says to you:
You look so beautiful
you smell so nice-
how I've missed you-
and did you come yet?

It means nothing,
and he is smaller
than a mouse's fart.

Don't listen to him ...
Go to Annaghdown Pier
with your father's rod.
Don't necessarily hold out
for the biggest one;
oftentimes the biggest ones
are the smallest in the end.

Bring them all home,
but not together.
One by one is the trick;
avoid red herrings and scandal.

Maybe you could take two
on the shortest day of the year.
Time is the cheater here

not you, so don't worry.
Many will bite the usual bait:
They will talk their slippery way
through fine clothes and expensive
perfume,
fishing up your independence.

These are,
The did-you-come-yets of the western
world,
the feather and fin rufflers.
Pity for them they have no wisdom.

Others will bite at any bait.
Maggot, suspender, or dead worm.
Throw them to the sharks.

In time one will crawl
out from under thigh-land.
Although drowning he will say,

"Woman I am terrified, why is the house
shaking?"

And you'll know he's the one.

Be Someone

(for Carmel)

For Christ's sake,
learn to type
and have something
to fall back on.

Be someone,
make something of yourself,
look at Gertrudo Ganley.

Always draw the curtains
when the lights are on.

Have nothing to do
with the Shantalla gang,
get yourself a right man
with a Humber Sceptre.

For Christ's sake
wash your neck
before going into God's house.

Learn to speak properly,
always pronounce your ings.
Never smoke on the street,
don't be caught dead
in them shameful tight slacks,

spare the butter,
economise,

and for Christ's sake
at all times,
watch your language.

Old Soldier

He stood
at the top
of Shop Street
cursing de Valera
and he muttered
something about
the Blueshirts
and when he saw
Mrs Flanagan, he said,
"You could have
got worse than me,
but you wanted
a fisherman didn't ya?
I wasn't always
like this," he said,
and his veins broke
and he died alone
but not lonely,
for many's the revolution
he fought in his scullery
with his newspaper
and his fine words.

His Mother was the Problem with his Veins

He wasn't old
but he couldn't
walk properly,
he tumbled
and stumbled
into other peoples'
dessert.
He fell into aftertalk
after dinner;
he talked about
after things
and after hours
and after mammy dies.

He wasn't old
his mother was the problem with his veins,
she tied them in knots
before he left the house;
she knew in her vein-tying heart
that he wouldn't get far,
no race was ever won
by the afterman
with his veins in a twist.

Her reasons were simple
The fruit of my womb

don't leave me Johnny,
you've had fifty five birthdays
(but only ten birthday cakes)

Don't grow out from me, Johnny
fruit of my womb,
be in at ten o'clock
and we'll have a look
at your veins.

Stop thinking Johnny
I have a bed full
of thoughts in my head
take from me,
I am your mother
your love
the one who ties your veins
for you.

And after that
all Johnny ever had
were more afterthoughts
about afterwords;

until one day
his veins started to bulge
from the side of his neck
the back of his knees
the ankles
around the curve

of his spine.
And he had a forethought
one evening after eight
about after mammy dies
about after mammy dies.

And he killed her
in his heart,
but he still stumbled
he often fell
he was still an afterman
meddling
in other peoples' afternoons.

And then she really died
dead dead died
into the ground died
late at night died
into the afterworld
she crawled afterdark;

leaving the fruit
of her womb
after her,
now sixty two
still an afterman
looking for birthday cakes
and a woman
to tie up after him.

I'm Strictly a Chair Person

(for Dr. R.D.)

Dear Doctor,
I have been trying
to reach you,
but every time
I try to ring
your door bell,
your savage Alsation
goes for me.

I wonder
if the fact
that I am
carrying an armchair
has anything to do with it.

My problem doctor,
It's nothing really,
I get emotionally involved
with chairs and things.

I'm not ill or anything,
but I know an awful lot
of sick chairs.

P.S. When we meet, is it o.k. if we stand?

Witch in the Bushes

(for Padraic Fiacc)

I know a man
who tried
to eat a rock
a big rock
grey and hard,
unfriendly too.

Days later
he is still grinding,
the rock
is not getting
any smaller.

Because of this
rock in the jaw,
this impediment,
the man has become
even more angry.

No one
could look at him,
but a few
hard cases did.
They were mostly dockers;
they reckoned,

"We have seen
the savage seas
rise over our dreams,
we can look
at a bull-head
eating a rock."

The years passed
slowly and painfully,
until one day
the rock was no more,
neither was much of the man.

He didn't
grind the rock down,
the rock
hammered a job
on him and his ego.

Then, one day
an old woman
came out of the bushes
wearing a black patch
and a questionnaire,
in her wand hand
she held a posh red pencil,
well pared.

She questioned him
between wheezes
(she had emphysema
from smoking damp tobacco
and inhaling fumes
from her open fire
in the woods)
if all that anger
for all those years
was worth it.

Old Rockie Jaw
couldn't answer
he had forgotten
the reason
and the cause.

He concluded,
"Anger is o.k.
if you spill it,
but chewing
is assuredly
murder on the teeth."

He had learned
his lesson
he would
pull himself together
smarten up like,

turn the other cheek,
he would go easy
on the oils that aged him.

Every now and then
he weakened,
he let the voice
from the rock take over,
an army voice
with a militant tone,

"A man is a man
and a real man
must spit feathers
when the occasion arises."

Like all good voices
this one
had an uncle,
it was the voice
of the uncle
that bothered him,
it always
had the same warning,

"About
the witch in the bushes,"
it said,
"Watch her,
she never sleeps".

79

Anything is Better
than Emptying Bins
(for Jessie)

I work at the Post Office.
I hate my job,
but my father said
there was no way
I could empty bins
and stay under his roof.

So naturally,
I took a ten week
extra mural course
on effective stamp licking;
entitled
"More lip and less tongue".

I was mostly unpleasant,
but always under forty
for young girls
who bought stamps with hearts
for Valentine's Day.

One day a woman asked me
could she borrow a paper clip,
she said something about
sending a few poems away
and how a paper clip

would make everything so much neater.
But I've met the make-my-poems-neater type before;
give in to her once,
and she'll be back in a week asking
"Have you got any stamps left over?"

Well I told her where to get off.
"Mrs. Neater-poems," I said,
"this is a post office
not a friggin' card shop,
and if you want paper clips
you'll get a whole box full
across the street for twenty pence."

Later when I told my father,
he replied,
"Son, it's not how I'd have handled it,
but anything is better than emptying bins."

Second Thoughts

It is better
not to tell
your best friend
that you have
a lover.

Because
in fourteen days
you might say
to yourself,

I should not
have told her.
Then you will go
to her house

even though
your shoes
are hurting you,
you will say to her,

my best friend,
remember
what I was telling you
fourteen days ago
at half past five,

well it's not true
I made it up
just for fun,
so forget
I ever mentioned it.

But when
you get to her house
you find
she is not in
in fact
you find her out.

So you go
to her place of work,
she works
at the sausage factory.

People
in a small group
at the main gate say,

"She is not here
and you
can't find her in
when she is out,
you must
find her out."

They tell you this
in a sing song way
she has gone
to the doctor's
they say it
four times
for no reason.

You wonder
if she
has told them,
you wonder
if they
are looking at you funny
and when you pass
are they saying
to themselves,
in their
older sisters' dresses,

"There she goes
that slut,
she should be
in the sausage factory,
she should be
a sausage."

By the time
you reach the doctor's

she has left,
you are sweating
on the road
through your clothes
into your
tight fitting shoes.

You wonder
if keeping your secret
has made her sick
and that is why
she is
at the doctor's.

You take the bus
to her house
you are there
before she opens
the front gate,

you are disappointed
when her mother
tells you
through their squint window
that she has gone back to work

to make up
the time
she lost

whilst going
to the doctor's
for a prescription
for her father's
catarrh.

You decide
there and then
to take out an ad
in the local paper,

telling her
to forget all you said
that Saturday
fourteen days ago
at half past five.

She is
more than pleased;
to your face
she tells you
the next time
you meet,

she adds to this
without blinking
that you won't mind
if she goes out
with the man

you never
had the affair with
as he had been
asking her
for seven months.

And you
look round the town
you have dragged
your dirty linen through

from her house
to the sausage
to the doctor's
to the mother's

And
you
look
up
and
down
the
long
narrow
streets
of
the
town

you
were
born
in
and
you
wonder.

He Fought Pigeon's Arses, Didn't He

And she pissed
in his toilet
and ate his sausages
and he said
there was nothing
but lust between them.

And on his day off
he got an aerosol
and he wanted to spray
the arses of dead pigeons black.

And he said to her
"If it's war you want
I'll give you war.
We'll have our own war,
spraying the arses of dead pigeons black
and we'll fight seven days out of six.

And the seventh day of the six
we'll discuss the situation,
and I'll bet you
twenty black pigeons' arses
there'll still be nothing
but lust between us."

I went to School with You

My children call her
Dolly Partners
and I don't check them.

Sometimes,
when I'm well fed
and satisfied in every other way
and they say it,
we all laugh.

One night when I was coming home
from Mick Taylor's, half pie-eyed,
she called me.

She had no pies in her eyes
and no flies either
she spoke with her finger
her index finger,
but she never danced with the afternoon
the sunny afternoon.

"It's your duty as a mother
to control your children",
said the finger, the index finger.

"When you are out,
(which is often," she muttered under her manacles)

"I can hear nothing
but Madonna blaring and your youngest swearing."
"And furthermore," said another voice,
in an Italian accent (but we couldn't hear it),

"You miserable hag,
you never speak with your finger
your index finger,
and shame on you
you often dance with the afternoon
the sunny afternoon.
How dare you, how absolutely dare you."

After that the finger came back on duty,
it was the index finger
and it was night duty
and it was her duty.

And the killing part of it all is, it said,

I went to school with you.

Oracle Readers

And we saw
what we saw
and we didn't see
what was hidden,

and we saw
that they were close,
they did everything
and nothing in unison,

they went for walks
they had talks
they went for tea.

Everyone
who sees them says,
"Look at the O'Hallorans
they are so cute,
would that we were them".

Once when they
were painting
the house
he got red paint
on his face,
he splashed her
so they would

look alike.
Everyone thought
they were cute,
we all said it together
at the crossroads,

"Aren't they cute
oh so cute
would that we were them."

Then one night
forty eight of us
crept up
to their bedroom window.

We heard him say
to his wife
his similar wife,

"Can I come inside you
tonight love?"
And she said
in a soft voice
in a similar voice,

"No dear,
not tonight dear,
three weeks
from now dear."

We were conned
by their cuteness,
they were not
as cute
as we thought.

After that
we wised up,
no longer
did we stand
at the crossroads
and shout,

"Aren't they cute
oh so cute
would that we
were them."

Our tune changed,
now we said,
"They fooled us
they fooled us,"

we were cock sure
he came inside her
every night,
but he didn't,
three weeks
from now dear.

94

We were fooled
we were conned
learn from us
and read
the signals correctly,

if a man splashes
red paint
on his wife's cheek
it means

he wants to come inside her;
if she leaves
the paint on
and smiles at him
all that same day,
that can mean
everything and nothing.

You think
that means yes,
we have a surprise for you
oracle reader,

the word
no for nothing
is forming
in her brain
and in her mouth,

while she is looking
at the stars
in his eyes
this no good,
no for nothing
will sneak out
and devour him.

Remember this
and learn
to interpret the paint splash,
and don't
get your signals
mixed up
at the crossroads,
like us
who thought we knew.

End of a Free Ride

For years
my cousin never charged me
on the bus.

One day he said to my sister,
"Your wan would need to watch herself
stickin' up for the knackers,"

After that he went home
and had pigs cheek and cabbage
lemon swiss roll and tea.

He called out to his wife Annie,
(who was in the scullery steeping
the shank for Thursday)

"Annie love get us the milk,
was I tellin' ya,
I'll have to start chargin' my cousin
full fare from here on in."

"Why's that?" said Annie love
returning with the milk

"Cos she's an adult now, that's why."

The Tell Tattler

Have you anything
to tell us today
tell tattler?

Did you help any
old woman across
a crowded street?

Did you spread
your Sunday coat in muck
for any dainty foot?

In a pub
spacious enough
for dreamers with hope,
not near enough
to Annaghmakerrig,
you can meet the tell tattler
with a gold pelican pinned to his lapel.

Without coaxing
or pain he will tell you
about the blood he has given over the years.

He was a school teacher once.
He put streams of children into his wife,

but they fell out again uneducated and sour.
In time they shouted
from sinking Monaghan hills.
"Where is our blood giving father now,
our chest pounder and coat spreader?
We no longer see his polished pelican
shining in the distance.

Your falling out children need to check:
that you have tells to tattle,
that you have an endless supply
of unwilling old women to drag across busy streets,
that you have cloth enough for the dainty foot,
that you have good hearing for when the bell tolls,
that you are not, our father, running out of blood."

Woman's Inhumanity to Woman
(Galway Labour Exchange)

And in this cage ladies and gentlemen,
we have the powers that be.

Powder power,
lipstick power,
pencil power,
paper power,
cigarette in the left hand power,
raised right of centre half plucked eyebrow, Cyclops
                                                power,

big tits power,
piercing eyes power,
filed witches nails power,
I own this building power,
I own you power,
fear of the priest power,
fear of the Black N' Tans power.

Your father drank too much power,
your sister had a baby when she was fifteen power,
where were you last night power,
upstairs in your house is dirty power,
the state of your hotpress power,
the state of your soul power,
keep door closed power,

keep eyes closed power,
no smoking power,
money for the black babies power,
queue only here power,
sign only there power,
breathe only when I tell you power.

No pissing on the staff power,
jingle of keys power,
your brother signs and works power,
ye have a retarded child power,
you sign and work power,
look over your shoulder power,
look over your brother's shoulder power,
I know your mother's maiden name power,
look at the ground power,
I know your father's maiden name power,
spy in the sky power,
spy in the toilet power,
fart in front of a bishop power.

Apologise for your mother's colour hair power,
apologise for your father's maiden name power,
apologise for being born power.

The Blanket Man

He calls
in his
new Volvo
collecting
the pound a week.

Him and his Volvo.

Sometimes
if she can't pay
he says,
"C'mon, c'mon missus,
if it was my stuff
I'd let you have it
for nothing."

Leaning against
the door jamb
she doesn't
believe him.

Her and her cigarette.

The Barmen of Sexford

In March
Sexford
can be as cold
as any
disappearing relative
with a toothache
you may find yourself
not siding with
in a hurricane.

The barmen
have no problem
with the cold,
they rip off your tights
with their fast
Indian bread breath,
never stopping
for traffic or history.

The people here
are warm
but black tights
means only one thing
to the men
of Sexford
the barmen of Sexford.

When you
clear your throat here
the barmen think
you are addressing them
they say,
"Were you
calling us just then
Black Legs,
can we
do anything for ya,
can we
shine yer knees
please, please?"

The comfort here
tumbled out
in hot whiskies
and a backbiting fire.

In Sexford
the fire was always there
but the barmen
didn't really exist
only in their mother's prayers
and in Communion photos
on the dusty mantle
beside the dead president
who was leaning against
the Sacred Bleeding Heart

and of course
in some kind old headmaster's
estimation.

Dog is Dog is Dog

"Xadore, come here
Xadore, don't urinate there,
not there, not anywhere here."

If that heap of failure
with the varicose face thinks
that us canines have
the same urinary tract
as those two leggers
she's got another thing coming,

                            on her ankle.

"Xadore, you stupid boy,
come here at once or you will fry."

Xadore exits to greener lamp-poles.

No Balls at All

The cats in Castle Park
are shameless,
they talk dirty all night long;
but not our Fluffy.

Our cat has been de-railed,
(that's Czechoslovakian for neutered)
but he doesn't know it.

He gets flashbacks
from his desire-filled past;
often along our back wall
he tiptoes tamely chasing pussy;

when he gets to the point of no return
he gets a blackout,
he well knows with his acute cat sense
that the next bit is the best bit;
but he just can't remember
what he is supposed to do.

He was an alley-cat-and-a-half once,
but felines complained,
not softly but oftenly
about his overzealous scratchy nature;

so we took him to the vet
where his desire was taken;
snapped at, whipped off, wiped out
by a man in a white coat.

It was sad really
de-railed in body but not fully in mind;
would he ever get over it?
Our cat with some desire and no equipment.

Days now
he just sits
inside our white lace curtain
envying his promiscuous alley-cat friends.

Other times,
he plays with a ball of blue wool
or a grey rubber mouse
throwing him in the air
letting on to be tough.

Still, he would have his memories,
they would come and visit him
teasing him back
to the tumbling times of testiclehood;

but sadly for the de-railed alley-cat
there is no second coming;
we came to accept it, and so did our Fluffy.

Sly Autumn

Sly Autumn
crept up my skirt
today
in Mainguard Street.

Peter Picasso

Feeding on
potatoes and onions
and heating himself
from stolen coal
and migraine memories
of a day flush with
carrot-weight friends
and apple song,
this Protestant painter lives.

"Take out someone's appendix
make someone's teeth sing
design a hideous church,
but for the love and honour
of all that is holy
stay away from the evil easel,
that's only for the death coloured
do-fuck-all dandified doters
who'd cut off your ear
as quick as they'd look at you".

Peter Picasso
who could well hear
but didn't listen
let his paint brush take him
to this chicken shite
wall world

next to Moo-hat post office,
where the crows ate the priest.*

His fall is broken
and so is his heart
when an art student in tight jeans
meanders through his chicken shite world.

He conjures her up
before and after feeds
and provided it's not too wet
and she swears not to step on his wolfhound,
she can glide with him
in and out of the heads of cows
and more things less political.

And on cold Winter nights
she can dance
on his stolen coal fire,
while he laughs at the walls
and checks that both ears are still there.

* A Christy Higgins line.

Some People

(for Eoin)

Some people know what it is like,

to be called a cunt in front of their children
to be short for the rent
to be short for the light
to be short for school books
to wait in Community Welfare waiting rooms full
                                        of smoke
to wait two years to have a tooth looked at
to wait another two years to have a tooth out (the
                                        same tooth)
to be half strangled by your varicose veins, but
                                you're 198th on the list
to talk into a banana on a jobsearch scheme
to talk into a banana in a jobsearch dream
to be out of work
to be out of money
to be out of fashion
to be out of friends
to be in for the Vincent de Paul man
to be in space for the milk man
(sorry, mammy isn't in today she's gone to Mars
                                for the weekend)
to be in Puerto Rico this week for the blanket man
to be in Puerto Rico next week for the blanket man
to be dead for the coal man

(sorry, mammy passed away in her sleep, overdose
                              of coal in the teapot)
to be in hospital unconscious for the rent man
                         (St.Judes ward 4th floor)
to be second hand
to be second class
to be no class
to be looked down on
to be walked on
to be pissed on
to be shat on

and other people don't.

Daughter of the Falls Road

*In memory of Mairéad Farrell,
murdered in Gibraltar, by SAS.
March 6, 1988.*

And the world heard
about the awfulness of it
and it got into
the minds of the people.

And it was bigger than them
and they feared it
they feared the bullet
and the bomb,
but mostly their own thoughts.

And in the minds of some people
were thoughts of pity
for the mothers of the three,
thoughts of anger
about the bullets to their heads,
and fear for their own flesh and blood.

And people wondered
why they were there,
and what strength of thought
propelled them, what conviction.

Some said,
tell me now
the politics of the dead,
some mentioned the struggle,
and other said,
the sun shines, we see no war,
but the Irish rarely
feel the sun;
they've heard about the war.

And from the eyes of her brothers
tumbled acid tears,
passing the place of their heart
seeping into closed fists,
and there was an acid tear ocean there
doing nothing. Waiting.

And in the minds of some people
came her mother and father,
they waited ten years,
now ten lifetimes won't bring her back.
Dead daughter of the Falls Road.

And there was talk
she had a boyfriend
who was tall,
whose acid tears tumbled
passing the place of his heart,
seeping into closed fists

and there was an acid tear ocean there
doing nothing. Waiting.
And in the minds of a lot of people
was the Irish girl
and her two companions,
brought home in boxes
made from Spanish trees.

And the living don't think
in tall straight lines
and Birch means little
when you're breathing
and in the hearts of some people
came another great wave.

And a lot now hate the Spanish trees
and the great hard Rock
the pitiless Rock
stealer of Irish youth.